BARBARA KERR

What is a baby ?

Edited by Richard & Helen Exley.
Parents and grandparents
describe the fun and frustrations
of bringing up baby.
Selected by Richard and Helen Exley
from the responses of
over 10,000 people — mostly mothers.

Exley Publications

By the same editors:
Grandmas and Grandpas (1975)
To Mum (1976)
To Dad (1976)
Happy Families (1977)
What is a husband? (1977)
Cats (and other crazy cuddlies) (1978)
Dogs (and other funny furries) (1978)
Dear World (1978)
A Child's View of Happiness (1979)
A Child's View of Christmas (1980)

Our thanks go to Dee Remington and
Woman magazine for all their help.

Our thanks for the front cover picture
go to GAF (Great Britain) Limited for
the loan of their photograph featuring
GAFSTAR 'Super-cushioned' sheet
vinyl flooring *Morocco* design number
22046.

Credits of model photographs:
Barnaby's Picture Library/Tony
    Boxall:33/T. Fellows:63/J. W.
    Rule:30/Jozef Vissel:48
Tony Boxall: 7, 19
J. D. Casey: 27
John Doidge: 5, 8, 9, 12, 22
Richard Exley: 51
Camilla Jessel:3,10,34,36,38,54/55,
    56,60
W. Millar:43
Claire Schwob:40
Anthea Sieveking, Vision
    International:15,17,21,49,52
Spectrum Colour Library: 24
Tony Stone Associates: 47

First published 1980 © Exley
Publications Ltd, 12 Ye Corner,
Chalk Hill, Watford, Herts, United
Kingdom, WD1 4BS.
Printed in Hungary by Kossuth.
Typeset by Beaver Reprographics
Ltd, Wiggenhall Industrial Estate,
Wiggenhall Road, Watford, Herts.
ISBN 0 905521 29 3

Reading the contributions received for What is a baby? vividly recaptured the memory of my own sons when they were younger. No other poems or books on this subject have ever had quite the same effect on me as these thousands of ordinary, genuine letters from parents and grandparents. Sometimes haltingly, sometimes searching for the right words, they made me relive the laughter, fun, chaos and occasional despair of being a young mother.

I hope the finished book has something of the same effect on you: whether you're contemplating motherhood, enjoying it, enduring it, watching it or remembering it. It's a fantastic subject!

My thanks go to Dee Remington and Woman magazine for helping to collect all the material, and to the thousands of families, published and unpublished, who helped by sharing their experience.

I dedicate the book to my own two sons, Lincoln and Dalton.

Helen Exley

What is a baby?

A baby is living proof that you've been a naughty girl.
June Johnson

A baby is the only time that one and one makes three.
Wendy Pagan

Two minutes after her birth, my husband said "That was easy, when are we going to have another one?" *Ruth Smith*

When I see the exhaustion of hassled young mothers, their lack of money, the humiliating, revolting jobs they do ... when I smell the smell and then look at their proud happy faces, then I know there must be *something* about babies. *David Porter, bachelor*

No one else ever needed me. Mind you, no one else ever peed on me.
Eileen Stower

Who cares if the Martians have landed or Liz Taylor has married again? "He took his first steps," or "He used his potty today," are the headlines in our house. *Barbara Adamson*

A baby is the friend of the washing machine manufacturer.
W. Simpson, father

A baby is buying him his first toothbrush for his first tooth.
Sue Johnson

You'll spend hours lulling a baby to sleep only to prod it awake soon after to make sure it's still breathing. *C. A. Wyatt*

A baby makes his mother sleep more lightly and his father appear to sleep more soundly. *D. Parker, grandparent*

A baby is happiness with a grin on his face and dinner in his hair. *R. Dobson, grandmother*

A baby is a pain in the neck. A constant supply of dirty nappies and sicky clothes. A continuous demand for feeds. A reason to keep you awake when you'd rather sleep.
Your baby of course, not mine. Mine's perfect. *W. Gerry*

A baby is someone who can't spell emancipation.

Deborah Heggie

4

More definitions

They are endlessly fascinating, utterly absorbing, and heaven to hand back to their parents when you have had enough!
Valerie Payne, grandmother

A baby changes your dinner party conversation from politics to poops. *Maurice Johnstone, father*

If a baby isn't being fed, you can bet he's being emptied.
Mrs Jephcott

I have seen grandads on all fours, and one has been seen seriously watching rugby on TV with a bucket on his head.
Margaret Kirk

The problem is that the paediatrician disagrees with the GP who disagrees with the health visitor who disagrees with the nurse who disagrees with your husband who disagrees with your mother-in-law who disagrees with your mother who disagrees with you. The answer is to agree with everyone and do what agrees with the baby. *Angela Lansbury*

Babies are beautiful, wonderful, exciting, enchanting, extraordinary little creatures — who grow up into ordinary folk like us. *Doris Dyson*

A baby is wanting to put the world to rights overnight, just for him. *Pauline Jansen*

A baby is God's way of saying the world should go on.
Doris Smith

A baby is the best cure for greed or selfishness. It's a lifelong cure that makes most Mums and Dads kind and human. The unlucky ones are the Dads who don't get knocked off their perches and stay chauvinists forever. *Julie Mapplebeck*

A baby is a blank cheque made payable to the human race.

Barbara Christine Seifert

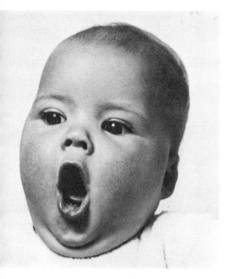

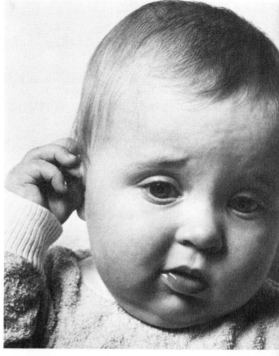

*It's the one thing no one really plans.
You plan a baby, and get a person.*

Linda McCutcheon

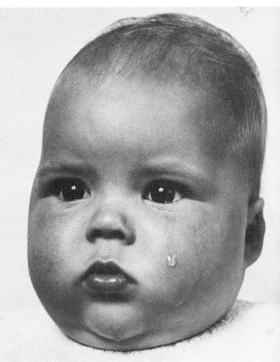

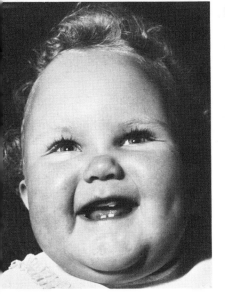

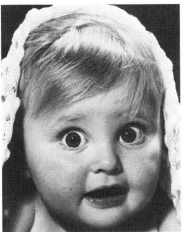

Demolition experts

A baby is something that stands on pet cats and dogs and then strangles them saying sorry.   *C. Greenhow, father*

A baby smiles disarmingly as he drops your last toilet roll down the loo.   *P. Dacey*

A baby puts her dismembered doll in the automatic, uses your best hairbrush on the puppy, wails in the middle of the night and laughs when you rush blearily in and trip over her pot in the dark.   *Clare Ryder*

A baby finds every grubby, germy thing to put in its mouth, when months have been spent sterilising everything and almost everyone on sight.   *J. Christie*

Life with a baby is never dull.   *J. L. Theed, grandmother*

What is a baby?
A sucking, grabbing, work
generating, sleep denying,
hyper-active,
mobile disaster bundle;
prone to the emission of
periodic excesses of decibels,
odours and noxious liquids,
that you wouldn't really swop
for anything in the world.
B. K. Taylor, father

A baby is the most lovable
automatic muck-making machine.
Pat Brown

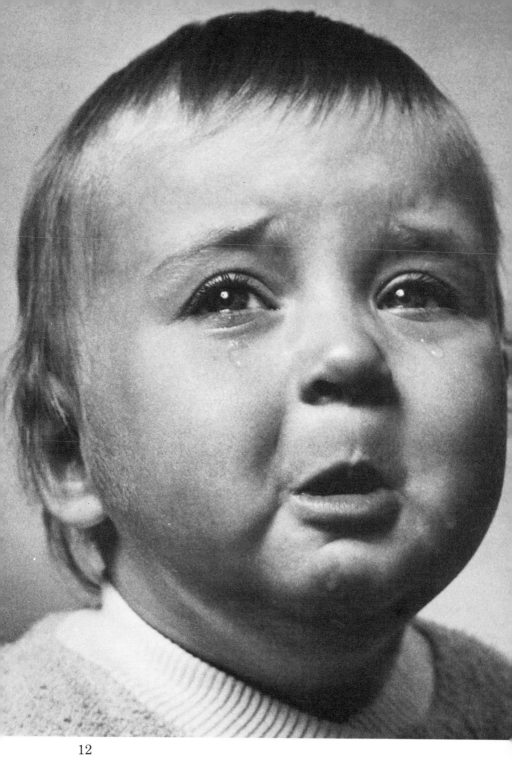

Wrapped around his little finger

When he is naughty, you spank him and make him cry, then cry yourself because you have made him cry.   *Susan Smart*

A baby can reduce a calm, intelligent, rational kindhearted male to a quivering wreck unable to combat a yelling red face above a wriggling squirming body. What is more a baby can do all this and then laugh right in the face of the sufferer — and get away with it!   *Joan Hill, grandmother*

She is a person who almost from birth can instantly recognise your weaknesses and coldly plays upon them to great effect. She learns at the tender age of seven months that crying may not bring instant attention any longer, but if she should cough, oh yes, if she coughs, that is something else.   *Colin French, father*

He is the luckiest person alive. He can have anything he wants. He knows how to please all of the people all of the time. He is not a poor, helpless, little mite. If he groans or whimpers, he can have a choice of a good meal or a complete change of clothes; when he wails or yells, he can bring in doctors, nurses, or any expert service he requires; and by forcing a bellow he can throw a whole household into a turmoil from which it may not emerge for several days. He can burp, break wind, drool and vomit — all to admiring and approving faces. Far from being helpless he is the person who makes best use of the world he lives in.
Mary Dickson

He seems to understand that whenever he cries and looks up at you, you're like putty in his hands.
J. Darbyshire

A baby is the only one who can win an argument without saying a word.
L. Lewis

13

A time for waiting

My unborn child
unfolding gently, like a flower.
I can feel you
slowly unfurling
though I cannot see you,
tiny but perfect.
Your heartbeat
so delicate yet so strong,
is the beginning of a new life,
unique in creation.
I can feel you.
I can hear you.
I cannot wait until
I can touch you
and see the smile of
my newborn child.

Susan Lewis

Love at first kick

A baby is, quite simply, a miracle. The fusion of two hearts, two souls, two bodies; two minute cells resulting in a miracle.
How does this cell, nourished by the mother's blood, multiply and differentiate to form a tiny individual?
Outwardly we see few signs. An amazingly expanding tum, the bloom of motherhood, tiredness, cramp perhaps and innumerable trips to the loo.
Yet within two hundred and forty days a baby will be born. A baby with perfect limbs and tiny digits. A beating heart, blood coursing through a complex maze of arteries and veins. Muscles, nerves, skin, hair, eyes, a tiny nose, mouth and a pulsating brain, with the ability to learn the skills of life.
There is no doubt that a baby is an everlasting mystery.

Susan M. Titterington, mother-to-be

A baby is a kick inside — a friendly, secret hello.   *Julia Belton*

A baby is holding one's stomach in the night to feel the flutterings and crying with joy and anticipation.

Jennifer Kattenburg

You can go (no longer under false pretences) into baby boutiques to touch the baby suits and smile insanely to yourself over the pretty cribs. Glorious hours can be spent unselfishly planning the nursery room — extravagance knowing no bounds. *AND* husbands approve.   *J. Clarke, mother-to-be*

A baby, the fruit of love, that tiny pip which you desperately want to grow big enough so that your partner can share these magic flutterings inside you. This little child-to-be even at this early stage has a personality and is christened 'bulge' by all and sundry.   *Yvonne Gardiner*

But best of all are those quiet moments, when I sit in the early morning sun and dream that my baby has arrived. He or she nuzzles my breast with clenched little fists and I can almost catch the perfume of my sweet little child. The dream is over for now and I look out onto the garden again, brought back to this world by the faint stirrings of my baby moving inside.

J. Clarke, mother-to-be

Two weeks to go and I feel fat and frightened. Before the bump I thought I loved my husband, but it was just puppy love.
Bump has brought us closer together, really welded us into one.

Sally Stoddart, mother-to-be

Pass quickly please you next few months.   *D. Brown, mother-to-be*

A baby is that great surge of joy when they tell you, "Yes your pregnancy test is positive." A baby is at last kicking away inside of me. I don't know him yet, but I love him.

Marian Cleworth

17

Family bonds

Most of all a baby is someone who makes the word 'bond' a reality.
Patricia Marsh

A baby changes an indifferent mother-in-law into a friend.
M. Owen, grandmother

A baby brings out the tenderness of the menfolk of the family.
W. Kirkpatrick, grandmother

A baby is understanding. Understanding, at last, how one's parents worried and cared. Understanding and forgiving what we thought were injustices in our own upbringing. *Val Sweeney*

A baby pays you back for all the things you did to your own mum!
Ellen Downie, mother of three

A baby is what makes a woman finally realise what her mother has done for her all her life. *Daphne Moss*

You're drawn closer to your mother because her grandchild is beginning to give you the anxiety lines that you give her.
Drina Parker

Life will never be the same again once a baby is born. A baby is pain, pleasure, tears. A baby is the passing of years, an unoccupied chair at the table, an empty bed. A baby is a warmth in the heart and a grandchild. But above all a baby is a family.
Angela Truscott, grandparent

He is all our tomorrows and some of our sunsets. He's got Uncle Fred's ears and great-grandma's nose. We all of us see what we want, I suppose. A baby is roots and the family united. We are all born again. The promise fulfilled.
Pat Garratt, mother of 3

My own baby daughter in her turn produced two boys and two girls, who, in the fullness of time have given me, up to date, six beautiful great-grands — and each one has a special place in my heart; and still they come, these little helpless bundles of love, made up of bonds and bands which bind and unite in a beloved bundle called a baby — a joyful miracle — wherein all labour is of love, the cost is not counted.   *Gwladys E. Oliver, great-grandmother*

You ask the question "What is a baby?" In my case (and I would prefer my name to be kept a secret between us) a baby brought me the most precious gift a woman could ask for. The friendship and, I hope, love of a stepdaughter who had been alienated from her father and myself for seven years suddenly became mine on the birth of her first child. He is nearly a year old and I have been privileged to see a new warmth and understanding blossom in our reunited family as he has smiled, cried and been desperately ill.
I have seen my man cry with joy on Christmas Day at the sight of his daughter and myself with our arms around each other, laughing at a baby drunk on champagne. It is a cliché, I know, but at least I know the meaning of the phrase, "God's gift to woman".   *Step-grandmother*

Birth, that personal miracle

The baby looks perfect and quite beautiful. I am speechless, words are not adequate. I feel the soft downy head on my arm, I can't believe it. Is this the climax of my dreams? For this delightful ecstatic moment I have endured the last nine months, and God knows how many years to come of misery and frustration. For surely one must pay in the end for such glimpses of heaven, surely one must *have* to pay? But there is no turning back, no trading-in of this fragile moment. This is nature's wily way, no escape, no will to escape, no desire to relinquish; just a fierce and violent love for this scrap of humanity. This feeling, I know, will remain after all others have long since given way to hopelessness.
I don't know if it's worth it, but I cannot help it. I am sacrificed, and there is nothing to be done about it. Nothing at all.

Brenda Bourhill

Total commitment, hopeless devotion and utter fulfilment. The thoughts in a mother's mind in those indescribable, totally personal few moments of first sight.
Afterwards, others enter the scene — beloved father, adoring grandparents, all happily shared, because deep down, a mother knows with almost reverent certainty, that this is the only totally honest relationship of mutual love and dependence. She knows, then, that this special event is unique in her life — that he will never again be completely 'hers'.
He will always have her love as he faces the good and evil of life, but a mother knows she will not always be able to protect him — that other people will make claims on his future. With sudden clarity she wants him to be loved and knows she will be able to let him go when the time comes.
But as she gazes at this tiny miracle, every mother reaches maturity.

Jennifer Elder

*"A boy," they say.
And tears course down my cheeks.
Quickly, the little body in my arms,
And with it
exaltation!
Such exaltation!*

Janet S. Saunders

20

Having a child is like reaching an unknown goal, as if all your being had been waiting for this moment. *Sheila Orrill*

Till the day I die I will always remember the joy of holding a new baby in my arms. *D. Duffy*

A baby is indeed the most beautiful miracle known to man, and it is a miracle which happens every day in life. *Nancy King*

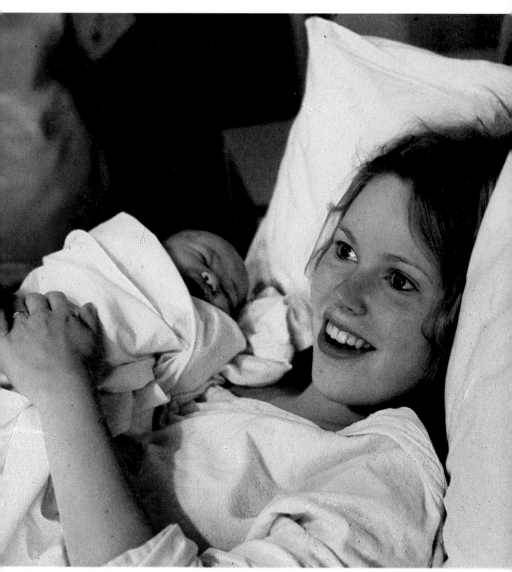

Innocence

Look into his eyes, 'the windows of the soul'. There are no curtains.
Mona Swales, grandmother

His age can only be counted in months as yet but already he has filled all our hearts with such wonder, such humility. We feel our hearts simply crumpling with tenderness towards this small scrap of humanity who already holds in his eyes all the freshness and innocence and joy of a new being setting forth into the world with triumphant delight which we hope will stay with him forever.
Margaret Smith, grandmother

A baby is innocence, purity and perfection in an increasingly guilty, impure and imperfect world.
Kathleen Shaughnessy

A baby is a warm, soft, silky being. Its innocence and vulnerability eats its way into your heart. It allows you the wonderful feeling of love and surrender. In return it demands that you give your heart, body and soul to protect and sustain it until it can fend for itself. Its very innocence is the armour it needs to survive. As a baby grows and thrives, so does the mother wither away. Such is the exchange of life.
Barbara Burdin

Why do we do it? Why do we inflict such devastation on ourselves? It is something to do with the pathetic beauty of the little face, the total innocence with which he demands the necessities of his life.
Alex Somerville

Babies are born innocent.
Dorothy Fiddes

We are a family now

I can't imagine what was so special about being a couple; being a family is so much nicer. *Alison McWilliams*

A baby is being amazed that you can be so unselfish and feel such love and tenderness — it's the tears that choke you when you see his dad holding him and realise that these two people turn on all the lights in your life. *Pauline Jansen*

When my man couldn't get a job, my baby made his shoulders proud and square again. *M. Smith*

He transforms a husband into a father, a boy into a man, in that same moment. *Jacqueline Marie Littlejohns*

Gone are the carefree days, we are parents, responsibility bears upon us. The children of yesterday are parents, the parents are grandparents; life has changed and will never be quite the same. *Janet McBeath*

I was married, after a nervous breakdown.
We managed on Social Security, and life seemed to have nothing but grey. After five years my daughter was born, and, still depressed, I looked at her in disbelief. Suddenly light and beauty entered my life once more. She was outstandingly beautiful and my body churned inside at the miracle. To us, who seemingly had nothing, had been given everything. One small baby has given us the strength to face tomorrow, and yet more tomorrows. Today, still poor, her every expression and unstinting love gives us all we need to go on. A baby's power has proved greater than that of any doctor to cure hearts and minds. *Susan Strachan*

A baby is a miracle,
a tiny person born to a woman
making her a mother
for the rest of her life
and her lover a father.
Maureen Sylvia Westwoods

A father is born

A baby turns a big hairy giant into a gentle humble Dad.
Roberta Edwards

A baby is flying arms and legs and a chocolatey kiss when Daddy comes home from work.
Marcia Lingard

A baby's arrival makes your strong unemotional husband weep with happiness.
Denyse Ponting

When you get home from a day with more than its usual share of disappointments and frustration and you wonder what it's all about, a warm little hand closes tightly over your finger and a broad smile of unaffected delight greets you. It is then you know that it's all about his tomorrow and to hell with your day.

K. J. Long, father

A baby is pacing the bedroom at three hourly intervals repeating that never to be forgotten plea, "Burp for daddy, there's a good girl. Burp for daddy."
Colin French, father

Before I became a father I never felt much for children... They were okay as long as they were behaved *i.e.* quiet. I had set ideas on how to bring up a boy from birth: "Lead with your left! Kick with your left foot!" Yes! with a boy I was on solid ground!
But I couldn't gauge my thoughts about a baby girl. All that changed for me when I left my wife and newly born daughter at the hospital, the night she was born.
I went to my wife's parents and told them there was something special about my little daughter. She wasn't just beautiful; there was .. something there! Now I know that 'something' is the love ... a special secret love a father has for his little girl ... a love that will cause more worries and pain, many moments of joy and eventually, the biggest lump I'll ever have in my throat, when she leaves her Daddy for her own man.   *Malcolm L. Miller, father*

The helplessness of a baby can turn a father's rugged work worn hands into the gentlest of cradles.

V. Bermingham

A new lease on life

I've a sneaky feeling that grandmothers get the best of it when it comes to a new baby. No long months of pregnancy — just a 'phone call giving the glad, glad news of the new arrival. The wonder never diminishes at the sight of the tiny hands and feet and the sheer helplessness of the new baby. But Nature has planned it well — babies are for the young and grannies give due adoration and handsome presents then go home to the happy prospect of an uninterrupted night's sleep. *M. Craig, grandmother*

The 20 month old baby in my life is the only person who could get this overweight, 58 year old, arthritic grandmother crawling around on the floor playing 'Big Roary Lions'.
Monica Shaw, grandmother

When you are a grandparent, a baby is an extra bonus of love sent to fill your empty arms, another chance.
Dorothy Simm, grandparent

Being a gran is compensation for my own babies becoming adults in a flash. I only blinked — honestly.
M. Harrison, grandmother

We hear screams of delight when they see me coming. "Nanny!" A big hug and kiss. We romp in the park, hop, skip and dance, it's tremendous. *I. Bull, grandparent*

A baby is a burp and a snuffle and the feeling of a soft little head burrowing into your shoulder, but better still, it's the eyes of a grandmother, it is a joy for years to come, a smiling face coming up the path for Saturday tea. It is the anticipation of the day when a little voice says so proudly 'That's my Nanna' and you feel ten feet tall, and the times when the head still burrows into you and says 'I do love you'. *Iris Peck*

To a grandmother a baby is a renewal of the life-force in a being whose innocence she prays that life will treat with kindness.
G. M. Green, grandmother

When you become a grandmother, it is like being a mum all over again, only better. *P. Parker, grandmother*

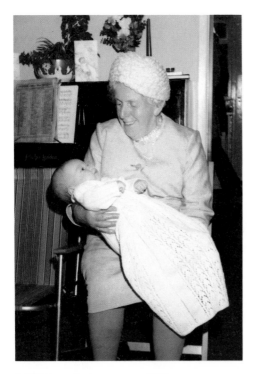

*"Would you like to see a snap
of our first grandchild?" Woe
betide anybody who doesn't!
Off with their heads!*

Anne Niels, *grandmother*

When I held my grandchildren as babies I wanted time to stand
still. *L. Mawson, grandma*

A baby is God's compensation to grandparents for growing
older. *J. Viner, grandmother*

Earthquakes, wars, terrifying epidemics — nothing stops birth.
Babies are born to scream defiance, to grow, to laugh and love, to
fill you with pride and perhaps to break your heart — but also to
give you hope that when you stop breathing you don't stop
living.
A bit of you goes on in a new baby. A baby to me is humble hope.

Florence Paris, grandmother to 5

If only time would stand still

I used to feel that if death came to me, I was ready. Life had been good to me. I felt satisfied.
Then came Jim. Now I grasp at life, hoping for just another day, another week, another Spring to watch him grow. Please don't let death come to me yet. *Alan Shawcross, grandfather*

Shortly before my first grandchild was born I had lost my beloved mother, and my grief was still locked within me.
One day I held my baby granddaughter, rocking and soothing her in my arms. Suddenly, the feel of her soft warmth seemed to touch a hidden spring. For the first time, the healing tears flowed, as if they would never stop.
Never have I felt such a wonderful surge of well-being and comfort as I did at that moment, brought to me through that baby. *Evelyn Velin, grandmother*

As a young mother, looking with disbelief, incredulity and shock upon the still-born face of my first daughter, I would have said a baby was misery and mystery.
Later on, lying in hospital with my second, perfect girl in my arms, not quite choirs of angels, but nurses in capes carolling by lantern light around our bed, a baby was joy, triumph, fulfilment. I was not to know then it also meant years of lasting love.
Learning that the three pound scrap of life in the incubator was my third, invalid, daughter, meant a baby was disaster. The six months of her life were a rage of grief, betrayal, rebellion and pure pain. Her death was part relief, part regret, wholly devastating.
I never saw a baby with my heart after that, so the first sight of my new-born grandson caught me unawares. My first impulse was to kneel. I would have said then that a baby was a small touch from the hand of God.
Now, with another happy laughing grandson to love, a baby is — what? Hope, perhaps, or promises? Or reassurance that there is some reason in the scheme of things.
What is a baby? It is Life, of course. What else?
Frances Mary Marston, grandparent

A grandchild is living proof that we loved each other so much, so long ago.

Brian Bloom, grandfather

He's my grandson

"Hello, how are you?" they say. "And how's your daughter? No family yet? How long have they been married?"
You reply "Oh — all in good time — not to worry." And then you think to yourself "Oh Lor' — all in good time, says me.
"Here am I getting on to eighty — can I see myself in three or four years' time going to the beach with my grandson — or granddaughter to build a sandcastle, digging a moat round it and then helping the sea to come and wash it all away, as I used to do when my daughter was his (or her) age?" Fancy an old white haired man digging in the sand like that. Not on your life! Well 'all in good time' *HE* came, and the miracle happened. Suddenly I was not nearly eighty, I was only seventy odd and quite capable of climbing into the loft to search for the wooden spade and the tin bucket. And tomorrow I will start off in the early dawn, when no-one else is about, and go down to the beach to practise sandcastle building again.
Oh! I know he is only five months old yet, but I can see it in his eyes, deep blue like the sea; in his fists opening and shutting to grasp the spade and his so perfect tiny feet getting ready to take him down to the sea to fetch a pail of water. There can be no doubt about it and I know in my heart, he not only will become the best sandcastle builder on the beach but 'all in good time' he will build, or help to build, a great new world, a perfect world, a clean, honest and peaceful world — built not on sand, but on rock.
I won't be there to see it but I have faith to believe that he will do just that because *he's my grandson.*   *Frank D. Murry, grandfather*

The anticipated arrival of his first grandchild was the inspiration behind Grandfather's total recovery from three consecutive strokes at the age of 75. His arrival has given Grandfather a daily incentive to be around for his first day at school.
Maureen Hallam

Eat it! <u>Please</u> eat it!

Feeding is comical at this stage. You need a shovel not a spoon. As soon as she's finished she wants more. If you wonder where she puts it all, look at her face and you'll find it.   *Léonie Dorey*

A baby is a little gourmet that happily digests Lego bricks, screws, the dog's biscuits and cigarette ends — only to turn up its nose at the chicken broth you've lovingly prepared. *Angela Bear*

A baby is eggy-soldiers, stuffed lovingly into the toe of my slippers; chocolatey-fingers run through my newly washed hair in affectionate abandon. Chewed and soggy shoulders on my best blouse. Squeals of delight at the sight of my sleek (well, almost) Afghan hound, with the remains of yesterday's Weetabix smeared with artistic precision through his long hair.
Judi Barnes

A baby is finding half a sausage in your purse.   *Carol Cooper*

How do you get banana out of the little holes in the 'phone?
Ann Miller

A baby is the urchin who wipes his sticky face on your dress, then hands you back his spotless bib.   *Rosetta Borland*

A baby has the manners of a wart hog.   *P. Dacey*

A baby is a fight with the chocolate pudding – with 'guess who' winning?
H. A. Evans

A baby is a clever boy because he's eaten the other half of the pudding you're scraping off the floor.
Margaret Airns

35

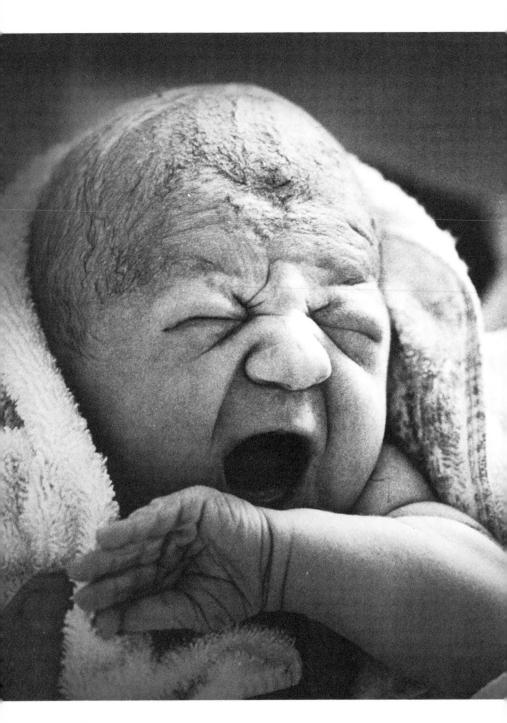

Ugly mugs

My dictionary gives as one definition of a baby "A grotesque decorative figure." They could be right.   *Judith A. Stephens*

They put it into your arms and say, "You have a beautiful baby."
This is a beautiful baby?
No hair, no eyebrows or eyelashes, a red face almost cut in half by a huge toothless mouth, and when that mouth first grabs your nipple you wonder if it is trying to suck you inside out. You spend your days putting food into the mouth only to have to clean it up from the other end. It screams and screams with wind in its tummy, so you hold it up on your shoulder and walk up and down rubbing its back, and of course, it rewards you by bringing up the wind and half its last feed all down your clean jumper. You feel like a slave to the little monster.
Whenever the grandparents visit it is lying asleep looking sweetly angelic, and they say, "What a good baby, so like Daddy used to be," not knowing that as soon as they turn their backs it will start yelling for its private robot to come running.
Then, one day, you go to pick it up and you realize it's looking at you, not past you or through you, but *at* you, and smiling and giving excited little wriggles because you are there. You notice other things too. It has grown eyebrows and long curling lashes, it has the beginning of fluffy fair curls on its head. You pick it up and feel soft little hands upon your face. That is when the real slavery starts. Before it was only physical, now it's mental too. But Mum you'll enjoy every minute of it, after all, haven't you just discovered you have the world's most beautiful perfect baby.
                                                        Eveline Waggett

*A baby is a funny little chap,
all wrinkled,
pink and noisy.*
Mrs Jephcott

Mini-dictators

A baby is a tyrant in knitted boots. *Torfrida Grieve*

Babies are the ones who start punching and kicking before they
are even born. *S. Ellison*

He's born with a wrinkled prune of a face, a frightened scrap of
humanity. But soon, with a thump of his fat, little fist, he's the
boss in every family! *Marilyn Stephenson*

A baby is nature's answer to the silicon chip — a small
component that governs the activity of a large machine.
Susan Griffiths

A baby is the tiny helpless bundle with the voice any sergeant
major would be proud of ! *S. Tidewell*

Ultimately a baby teaches you that adults teach you nothing. There is only one rule to remember concerning babies — he rules. Never have so many people done so much, so often, for one so small.

Angela Lansbury

He is tyrannical. He combines the charm of Rudolph Nureyev with the iron determination of Winston Churchill.

Anne Hammond

He expects his work force to be dedicated to the company, hard working, unswervingly loyal and highly efficient — while he takes care of the important side of the business — food intake. He refuses to tolerate unrest. Strikes in his brilliantly well-managed industry are unheard of and he expects his employees to be first class.

But job satisfaction is so high that more and more people are going in for this special creation programme. And remuneration for the deserving employee is ample when he is allowed to bask in the toothless smile of the mogul!

Lynda Alison Dunlevy

He makes inhuman demands of his devoted attendants, who totter from day to day in a blur of exhaustion. But how can they refuse to serve their mini-maharajah? After all, he's only a baby.

Anne Hammond, mum of five

A baby needs food, warmth, and love, and he knows exactly where to get it from - you!

Christine Armstrong

When hungry, he is a screaming scrap of humanity, with flailing arms and legs, crumpled face, as lined as an old man, furiously indignant that mother or father can't move faster with bottle and food.

Erica Rolls, grandmother

Nobody said it was like this!

People said I'd slim down quickly. Nobody told me it was because I'd never have time to eat. "You'll never have anything to wear," they all said, but didn't tell me it was because I'd never get out of a dressing gown till midday. "Sleep when baby sleeps," suggested the clinic. "When's that?" I asked. Never have I felt so wretched with tiredness. My hands are like emery paper and my nails non-existent. Never has so much been sterilised and never has the house stunk so much with sick, and why, oh, why haven't I got shares in Kleenex?

"Now Mrs D, don't have your second too soon", said the doctor. No chance, thought I, we haven't the energy to kiss one another goodnight. A baby? Undying sacrifice.

A baby means you are no longer an independent person in your own right, you are Basil's wife, or Wendy's mum, seldom just you.

I look back to when my baby was tiny with bitter memories. I welcomed the chance to tell you what I think a baby is. I wasn't going to paint a rosy picture, as everyone else who writes to you will do. I was going to expose the biggest cover-up since 'Watergate' — the myths surrounding babies perpetuated by advertising, baby books, etc. They do not tell you that a baby may take two hours to take each feed, day and night (as mine did). How lonely and isolated you feel after working with people for thirteen years. You are not told that sheer exhaustion takes away any joy you should gain from your baby.

Yet I feel guilty while writing this, as I remember the first time those two piercing blue eyes looked at me, and I knew I would love her through all the hardships. *All names withheld*

Having a baby is the biggest shock, the biggest eye-opener that any unsuspecting young woman will ever have in life. Its demands are so total that unless you have lived through it, it is impossible to imagine.

A classic sense of timing

A baby is the best form of birth control — he always wakes up in the night just as your husband cuddles up to you.

Carole Tabbron

A baby is 4 am and sandpaper eyeballs searching wearily for the last teat, which has just shot across the kitchen.
A baby is 5 am and helpful husband to prone spouse: "I was going to change him for you but it's one of *those*, so you'll have to do it."

Jean M. Horsham

It didn't take him long to work out my bed time. Graciously, he allowed me to drift into a relaxed doze. Then he would tune up with a series of whimpers. Silence. Next, a few more whines in practice, followed by the whole crashing symphony of screams, delivered with all of the vigour of a world class orchestra in full swing.

Elizabeth Ward

Babies have subtle ways of making mothers feel foolish. A baby's rash disappears at the doctor's. He grizzles all afternoon until you phone mother-in-law in desperation. When she rushes in he greets her with a grin. He refuses to eat mother's delicious, nutricious egg custard but chews a plastic bib with obvious satisfaction.

Angela Lansbury

A baby is the chatterbox who refuses to talk to your visitors, then engages in deep conversation with the dog.

Rosetta Borland

Our son promptly sicked on his Dad's boss. He has always been loyal but thank goodness he has now learned to hide the family's feelings.

Victoria Holden

Baby will look so beautiful when you set out for a day's shopping up in town, you feel so proud, until he dirties his nappy and shouts, "Poo!" at the top of his voice.

Laurie Benton

A baby is outstretched hands and calling "Daddy" to every strange male you meet.

Rita E. Charlick

A baby frowns at the camera then laughs as soon as it's put away. *Vanessa Davies*

A baby is someone who can stick out his tongue at people he doesn't like and be told how cute he is. *Pauline Jepson*

A baby is a human being that can wet himself, throw food at the wall, and scream in the middle of a crowded shop without feeling in the least self-conscious. *Dena Williams*

A baby is someone who rescues one from boring, gossip-ridden coffee mornings, by shouting "vroom," "vroom," then crawls to my handbag, brings my car keys, and waves them under my nose as he climbs on to my knee, still shouting "vroom," "vroom." *Jill Flemming*

A baby is someone who is allowed to batter *you* in public. *P. de Waal*

A baby is never being able to sneak off to the toilet without hearing a little voice saying "Good boy, Mummy." *P. Ormesher*

Goodbye Women's Lib!

A baby makes you feel that someone is eventually going to report you to Women's Lib for actually admitting that being at home and tied to nappies and the kitchen sink can be as rewarding as a career. *Diana Clifford*

A baby was the last thing on earth I wanted, but when he entered into my life I fell hopelessly and completely in love for the very first time in my life. He stood for everything I had hitherto despised. He was vulnerable and dependent yet he filled me with an awareness I did not know existed. I was actually glad to be a woman and suffer the so-called indignity of giving birth.

I have to be honest and admit there are times when he has driven me to distraction, and I have wondered why I forfeited my freedom for such a little monster but I have only to look at him in all his innocence to know I made the right decision.

I may give him food, warmth and security but he has given me much more. Through him I have learnt to appreciate the value of life. If he were ever to be taken from me my whole being would be filled with a despair from which I doubt I would ever recover. *Anne Patricia Lewis*

I can find no words to explain how motherhood succeeded in changing me. I who prided myself on being a sophisticated intellectual, with no interest in babies and a strong determination never to sink into domesticity, was transported into a world in which my children are the most vital part of my whole existence.

It is a world in which I have experienced heights and depths of emotions that I never even imagined, an enchanted world in which I have moved backwards to recapture the wonder and magic of childhood, and forwards to grow up to meet the needs of my new role. It is a world in which I can never again be free, and would never want to. *Yetta Peterson*

Your lives of Dr. Johnson are replaced by works of Dr. Spock, you find not one of Shakespeare's sonnets equal one "goo-goo". And you ask yourself "Where went that other woman — the career type, the cynic?" *Bernadette Hegarty*

Each baby is a nail in the coffin of Women's Lib.

D. J. Hopson

44

A baby changes a rather self-centred woman who enjoys using her leisure time for lazing around, making herself beautiful, reading or watching television into a nurse that looks after him twenty four hours a day, coming to attention with his first squeak.
But the strangest thing is that although she has completely lost her personal freedom she has never been happier in all her life now that she is serving her baby. *Uta Reed*

Achievement

A baby is the realisation that two very ordinary people can create a miracle. *Annette McAllister*

I was, now am again, a business executive. In between, I had two babies. Being a mum was more tiring, more difficult, more tense-making.
I didn't often achieve a state of organisation and I found it more stressful than doing financial deals or coping with masses of appointments. I'm not complaining — it was the greatest thing, the most creative thing, the most beautiful thing I've ever done. People admire me for my achievements as a business woman. I know that my greatest achievement was being an ordinary mum. *Helen Thomson*

Many men dream of the responsibility of scoring the winning goal in the Cup Final or hitting the runs which win a test match. I scored my Cup Final goal eleven years ago. "Justine" we called her. Four years later I hit that winning run and we called him Simon. *Michael L. Pearce, proud father*

You can paint a masterpiece like Picasso, create a new hairstyle, an exclusive gown — but whether you are rich or poor, black, yellow or white, the most intriguing fascinating creation of all is a baby. *Jennifer Jackson*

In the modern world of electronics and 'micro-chips' the birth of a baby is as much a miracle as it was in the stone age.
John Taylor, father

45

Suddenly it's all worthwhile

Another cold grey winter's day dawns. I awake and contemplate the dreary day ahead — feeding, bathing, nappy changing, endless washing. Wearily I stumble out of bed into the baby's room. Two bright eyes shine in recognition and a smile beams across that tiny face, as if the sun has peeped from behind the dark clouds. Suddenly everything seems so worthwhile. I feel I am the luckiest woman alive.   *Jennifer McNish*

The whole world may think you're a no-one, not much to look at and hate your jokes but your baby will stretch her little arms out to you, smile at you and laugh at all your silly talk. Her legs will kick with delight when you are near. You're her No. 1 and you love her so much it hurts.   *A. Bates*

A new outfit becomes a luxury. No more evenings out — you can no longer afford a candlelit dinner for two, even if you can find a babysitter. And certainly no more holidays abroad. A new car is out of the question.
And yet, as you watch him now making his way from the cat food to the coal bucket, and he pauses briefly to flash you the wickedest of grins, you know that he is so bloody innocent — it's not his fault he was a mistake — and you love him so much you wouldn't send him back, even if you could.   *Jacalyn Knowles*

My proudest pleasure is when my beautiful little three-year-old girl puts her arms around my neck, she squeezes me tight and says "I love you mummy, I really do."   *A. Cooper*

A baby plunges your home, career and social life into total upheaval, and then, as you sit shattered in the midst of all this confusion, the baby burps milkily, and falls into a peaceful, well-fed sleep, and you gaze at it, and feel an enormous wave of admiration and pride, and the gentlest love, and wonder that you doubted for a minute, how amazingly fortunate you are ... to have a baby.   *Barbara Strong*

At the end of the day, you climb (or rather crawl) up the stairs, convinced you will see two little horns poking out from under the bedclothes. But instead, there she is — a little angel— beautiful, clean and asleep. Then you want to wake her up and cuddle her!
                                                        S. Iwaniszyn

When at last the day is through you stand exhausted by the cot, and see your baby asleep — at peace with you and all his little world. You gaze at the most beautiful sight in the world — *your* baby, beyond price, sleeping peacefully — wrapped in love and security.   *D. Duffield, grandmother*

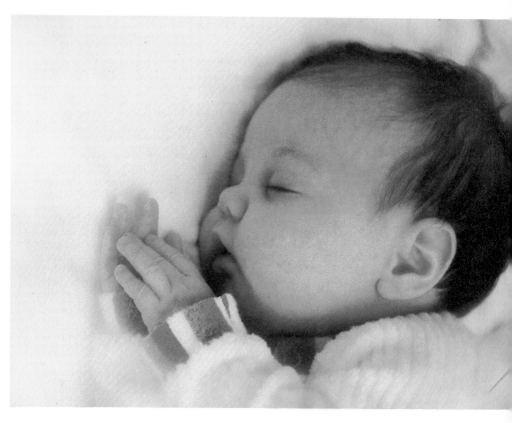

*A baby is the tightness
you feel in your throat
when you look in on them
fast asleep in their cots.*

Christine Blakemore

Something physical

Have you ever put your lips to the nape of a baby's neck? If so you will have felt the warmth and softness, not to mention the baby scent even Chanel couldn't imitate. *M. Clayton*

Every fascinating detail from the large liquid eyes, to the tiniest toenails, is unbelievable in its perfection. *Joan Rix*

That skin. Like a soft cloud made touchable. That indefinable fragrance. Like a new kind of flower. Those tiny fingers. Unbelievable in their perfection. Those little toes, the undersides of which feel like a row of the sweetest peas. To hold that warm, sweet bundle in your arms is bliss. *M. J. Ellis*

A baby is gazing in wonder at twenty tiny fingers and toes. *Frances Oakendon*

A baby holds tightly to your finger with a strength that will amaze you, but will clutch weakly to your breast and if you hold the soft body close to you, you realise how fragile this tiny being is. *L. M. Bishop*

Once that tiny hand has gripped your finger you are his slave for life. *Florence Berry*

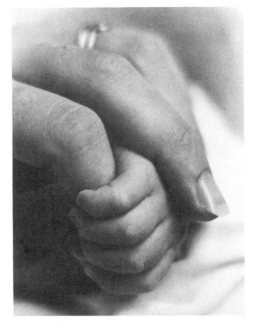

All irritations are brushed aside when that little mouth nuzzles into your breast and those chubby fingers clasp your own.

Valerie Skilling

Who teaches who?

A baby is the 'on' switch that releases and allows us to give full rein to all those emotions of tenderness, protectiveness and compassion, without appearing ridiculous to the rest of the world. *Barbara Christine Seifert*

A baby is the wisest and most liberated member of the human race. He sees a wonder in the commonplace, yet knows no difference between common and rare. Unfettered by ambition, not yet having learnt to pursue power, material gain or worldly success, his priorities are few, yet who would dispute their precedence: love, food, shelter, warmth, care? *Andrea L. Crozier*

In the long term, having a baby changes you so fundamentally that you can never again exist solely for yourself. *Ilana Wooster*

A baby takes your calm orderly life by the scruff of the neck and shakes it until you can see clearly what life is all about. *Cathy McLelland*

There is nothing better for the soul than changing a nappy. Such a basic and humbling task seems to put everyone and everything into perspective. *Sue Marshall*

They teach us so much, like the important things we sometimes forget: innocence, being happy with ourselves, doing simple things and getting enormous pleasure from them. They soften us inside and bring out all the love that we sometimes mightn't demonstrate too much. *Marie McQuade, aunt*

Parents and schoolteachers despaired. I was so selfish. No one could change me. Then came my babies. Since then I've been cured. No nagging needed. I can love and give.
W. Brierley

Babies are the biggest incentive to live and act decently.

Doris M. Bridge, grandmother

Each day my baby amazes me more, not only with her cleverness and beauty, but with the person I have become because of her.

Margaret Atkinson

A baby is a new meaning at Christmas, as you enjoy all the things which only months before you classed as commercialized.

S. Tidswell

A baby is the realisation that living for someone else is more fulfilling than living for yourself. Its very existence motivates a failed life into conquering that failure.

Hannah King

Babies are here to remind us that we're human.

Jonathan Shields, father

Joy, friendship, laughter

A baby is a miracle of life unfolding before one's eyes. It is akin to watching a slow-motion film of a bud opening into a flower, and a baby invites one to share each precious moment at a natural pace. There is laughter and there are tears to compare with sunshine and rain. The beauty catches the heart of anyone prepared to observe. Most of all the baby's love, like the beauty of the flower, is given unconditionally with a trust and faith that it will not be bruised or spoiled. Within its influence people find that they themselves respond by becoming more loving.

Elizabeth Williams

He teaches us the glorious *fun* of being alive. *Jacqueline Fletcher*

The love and happiness a baby brings are all free. There is no
charge. *N. Wood, grandmother*

A baby is the beginning of a beautiful, unending love affair, with
all its happiness and pain. *Pauline Elliott*

A baby is a way of seeing, feeling, for real. *Lesley Potter*

A baby can transport us into another world — away from
inflation, greed and violence; and leave us laughing. *Kay Sharp*

My eldest daughter saved my life twenty-four years ago. She was
only eight months old when her Daddy died, under very tragic
circumstances. My dear old Mum was around to take us both
under her wing, but it was my baby who sat on my knee for hours
while I poured out all my troubles. With her innocent little face
gazing up at my tear-stained one, day after day, I told her how we
couldn't go on without Daddy, but every day she gave me a new
reason for going on. Her first words were still "Dad-Dad".
Barbara J. Windle, grandmother

To me, as a profoundly deaf mum, baby is the best reward. She
breaks all the barriers between herself and myself and I feel ten
feet tall when she waddles up to me for comfort or to play or just
to talk. She understands my flat deaf voice. *P. Jill Palmer*

According to Barrie, beloved of the fairies, "When the first baby
laughed for the first time the laugh broke into a thousand pieces
and they all went skipping about and that was the beginning of
the fairies."
A baby is magic. *C. C. Graham, grandfather*

. . . All young things are the joy of the earth.

B. M. Yeoman, grandmother

A baby is just the best reason there is for simply being alive.

C. W. Bentley

Through the eyes of a child

A baby is seeing for the first time — clouds scudding by, trees moving, big red buses, tiny insects.
A baby is hearing for the first time — rain drumming on the window, birds chattering, a dust cart clanking down the road.
A baby is feeling for the first time — the soft fur of a cat, hot sun and cold snow, water rippling and splashing.
A baby makes you feel every emotion more deeply than before. Your tears are more distraught, your worries more desperate, your fears more panic stricken. Your laughter is warmer, your smiles more tender, your love unbounded.   *S. A. Playforth*

Augustus is someone to show the world to for the first time, that the garden is a wonderful place, the kitchen even more fascinating and bathtime is splashtime with a capital S!
Sue Bradbury

A baby will make all Christmases what they always should be, will help you to rediscover the light of a birthday candle, the softness of a small chick, the fact that snow falling means birds' traces and snowmen, not only train delays.   *Nathalie Lloyd*

A baby is the greatest
teacher of all;
he teaches you how
to find joy in all the
simple little things in life.
D. Brown

A baby is your instant introduction to women of all ages, everywhere. Suddenly the world is full of friends.

Angela Lansbury

A baby is joy, laughter, happiness, heartache, tears — the essence of all that is basically human in all of us and with which we can all identify. It can make us or break us, and in the process we realise our own strengths, our own weaknesses and perhaps more important, we reach out to the rest of mankind and understand their strengths and weaknesses too. *M. A. Rogan*

Child of our world

He is a reminder because he is all the children of the world, growing on this earth, with rightful expectation of love and peace. He reminds me what sort of world we should be striving to create for him.   *Dominic Quarrell, father*

Papoose, bambino, brown, white or black, a baby knows no colour prejudice. Whatever his race he is the most precious gift anyone can ever hold. If one is lost he can never be replaced, no matter how many others may follow.   *Linda Dyer*

His sad old eyes gaze out, remotely, from your television screen; a hungry, anxious face. Pot-bellied and wasted, he clings to his dark-skinned mother with her apathetic face and milkless breasts. Far away in his under-developed country he may die from disease or malnutrition, before he is two years old. But he too is a baby. Please do not forget him.   *Joan M. Souper*

A baby is the deepest emotional experience that can happen to a woman. Because of this it creates a fascinating bond between mothers of all ages, creeds and colours. A mother can stand with her child and look to all past generations of mothers with sympathy and understanding. She can look across the world and be at one with all who share her experience. She can share the agony of the bereaved mother, the anxiety of the mother with the sick or handicapped baby and also, with a good deal of concern and imagination, the terrific sorrow and heartbreak of the mother who, because of poverty or famine, is watching her baby die of starvation. She can look to the future and know that for all of time, all mothers with babies will share something of that which she has known and experienced – because of her baby.   *Joyce Young*

A baby is understanding mothers everywhere. Mothers coping with illness, with starvation, with war. A baby is one's entrance, at last, to the human race.
Val Sweeney

Adopting a baby

After years of waiting, it was not a rush to the nearest maternity ward, but a rush up the M4 from Wales to Heathrow Airport where my husband and I experienced the most wonderful moment of our whole lives.

Amongst the rush and turmoil of the airport, we were handed our darling baby son David, a war orphan from Cambodia. The joy of that moment? There are not enough adequate words to describe. In the middle of the busy airport, it was as if the three of us were cut off from the rest of the world. Tears of joy running down our faces, as we realised we really had our baby.

Back home we kept pinching ourselves and going into his room just to make sure we were not dreaming. The wonderful moments went on, with the smile and the outstretched arms to come to you, because you're his mum and dad and he knows. His first "Dad Dad and Mum Mum." Just to see those toys left about on the floor when you have just tucked him up in bed.

Baby David made our lives: this house is so full of love.

Janet Thomas

A baby is heartache and happiness. Heartache for the young unmarried mother who gathered together a trousseau of nappies, baby dresses, knitted jackets, a squeaky toy and instructions on feeding. All these packed into a box for her baby daughter, who was brought to us, her adoptive parents after six years of waiting.

The children's officer walked up the garden path with the baby in her arms; the box followed behind carried by a colleague. The baby was placed into the carrycot which was waiting for her — and there was our happiness.

Six months later a red robed judge pronounced her our first born and happiness was complete.

We hope that *her* heartache was eased. *Margaret Watson*

Without a husband

When your husband has left you for someone else, and tranquillisers are swallowed daily, helping you cope with a lively 17-month-old teething baby, the only thing that makes the long lonely nights and days worthwhile is when you get that little bundle out of his cot, with arms and eyes uplifted, he says, with a toothy loving smile, "Mum, up!", planting a kiss on your cheek and a big cuddle.

How can this fail to lift your heart above the depths of lonely one-parent despair, giving you hope for the days ahead. There is something to live for. There is him. There is love.

Name withheld

A baby is the one thing you still have that is part of both of you even when your marriage has broken up.   *Barbara Collings*

I'm an unmarried mother who was advised by almost everyone to have her adopted. Every day I look at her and thank God I didn't. She is a child of the universe no less than the trees and stars, she has a right to be here.   *Annette Louise Warburton, single*

Never having a baby

A baby was the ideal of my teens; the happy hope of my twenties; the sad frustrating longing of my thirties, and the fading dream of my approaching forties. My baby was not even conceived but how very much I longed for it and how infinitely precious and loved it would have been.   *Helen Hopkins, no children*

I have been married 42 years, and was never lucky enough to have a baby, but wish with all my heart that I had. It's been a great emptiness in my life.   *Edna Jackson, no children*

A baby is something I wish I could have more than anything else in the world. (I hope God reads this.)   *Sharon Cain, no children*

Bereavement

A baby is a hazy feeling of softness, a picture in my memory forever — for baby was only lent to us for six short weeks and gone before any photograph could be taken. Just a tiny white coffin in which our only son was laid to rest and a tiny cluster of snowdrops by his side.
A baby is . . . a sad but beautiful memory.   *Jill Marjorie Pounds*

He was a mongol child and he died on my birthday, 22nd January. The pain defies words but baby still means beautiful.
      Sheila Brown, mother of Samantha, age 2, whose twin
      died just after birth.

A baby is an old chocolate box of memories: the tiny pink bracelet put on Jenny Marie at her birth on the 4th January. The cards of congratulations to the proud parents. The hairbrush which I lovingly used for eleven weeks and one day that Jenny was with us. The letters of sympathy sent at her sudden death. The notice in the local paper. A few very precious photographs of the happy moments we shared. A leaflet from the hospital offering us help and telling us that we were just one of the thirty parents in the country who, in that week of March, would suffer the unexpected death of their babies.
      L. J. Wing, bereaved mother

Journey to independence

A baby is a traveller in time. From fragments of yourselves, you have created someone utterly new and unlike any other. She is someone who sets off this first morning on a journey. You can only accompany her a little way, for she is bound for a time you will not see, springs and summers beyond your knowing. She is so small, so dependent upon your care — yet she is a summary of all the centuries that have passed since the world began. She holds the key to all the knowledge man has harvested, to all speculation; and she is filled with the old, insatiable desire to learn. She lies so quiet in your arms, yet she carries the seeds of creation, mankind's obsessive need to make — cathedrals and bread, bridges and laws and hundred-foot murals. She is your own dearly loved child, yet every second takes her further from you.

She wants so little — warmth, food, love — but she seeks them with an urgency and determination out of all proportion to her tiny body. For she has somewhere to go, something to do, preparation to make for her voyage. Do not love her as a possession or she will break your heart. She is already beyond your understanding — and yet, something of her will always need those first things — warmth and food and love. She is learning from you how to give them as well as how to take. All generations fail, yet something endures, some little gain to pass on as a legacy with all the debts the young inherit.

That fraction of yourselves you gave goes with her into the huge darkness — which for her is full of light. The shadows of her ancestors whisper in her mind. She is herself and yet a galaxy. Each child explores its parent's mysteries and finds them commonplace. No creature is so frail or so afraid — or moves with such enormous courage into the unknown.

She is so very small. Around her space and time dance out their slow mathematics. Certainty recedes forever. Yet she is more than any mindless star. Love her.   *Pam Brown*

. . . For she has somewhere to go, something to do, preparation to make for her voyage. Do not love her as a possession or she will break your heart.

Pam Brown

A sacred trust

"Dear God — What a responsibility, but thank you *very* much."
Joan Mary Jones

A baby is a clear, unblemished page on which we can write anything we fancy — God guide us to use the right words.
Minnie Haman, grandmother

He is yours to hold in your cupped hands, to guard and to guide. Give him your strength and wisdom and all the good that life can offer. Yours is a sacred trust. Never harm him with words that bite and sting. Lead him into truth. *Veronica Read*

This tiny little being is one in a great big world to be cared for and taught as best as you know how; then, like a seed growing, this little pink bundle which you have planted will grow stronger with each year that passes. We must treat baby gently and wait patiently for each achievement, each word, each step and praise him. Let him know he's loved and important in this great big world of ours. *Sally Penn*

Only on loan

Babyhood is so short. It should be savoured and enjoyed, as the beauty of a dragonfly on a Summer's day, so quick in its passing. It's been and gone in a blink of an eye.
Barbara Freer

A baby is something you carry inside you for nine months, in your arms for three years and in your heart till the day you die.
Mary Mason

He came, vulnerable and naked, fists clenched in a ball.
He went, trained and cared for, strong and tall.
And in the years between, I thought him my own,
Refusing to see he was only on loan.

He grew and matured, till at last he stood free,
Unshackled, he had no more need of me.
And then he was gone, and the silence around
Left me deafened and deadened, with echoing sound.

Now, as I watch his young wife, with her babe in embrace'
And I see the proud smile on her sweet gentle face,
I think of that hard task she yet has to know
Not when to hold fast,
But when to let go. *Josephine Fuller, grandmother*

A baby is understanding one's mother-in-law too. We realize that she has passed her child over to the care of another. We understand her loss and know that one day we will feel the same way.
Val Sweeney

A baby is a problem that takes sixteen years to solve. How to fill the next sixteen years is now the problem.
Mrs Keele, grandmother

He will grow up and away from me to make his own way in the world and I must let go. But for the moment I make the most of every precious moment.
My wonderful, perfect little bundle of fierce emotions. My little man.
O. M. Rodrigues

He may achieve greatness by some physical achievement or earn the respect of the world through discovering something that will benefit mankind for evermore. He may become a man in a man's world — but to the woman who gave him life he will always be her baby.
R. Davies, grandmother

A baby is a feeling of tenderness so deep it knots your tummy. You wish you could take all your feelings and bottle them forever.
T. M. McCarthy

You love him forever, whatever he may do.
J. A. Mabbs

You'll let him go, as you always knew you would. For even as that pink and purring baby he was his own possession, not yours. And letting him grow away from you is the only way to hold his love.
Pam Brown

63

Some interesting ideas for gifts